Skillfully translates complex scientific concepts into accessible plain English, to provide a practical understanding of resilience.

Riley Desai, senior director of human resources

Explores themes of resilience, positive psychology, emotional intelligence and mindfulness, providing valuable insights in a clear and engaging manner.

Avery Chen, EVP of global marketing

Gently inquisitive, engaging and supportive. This book will change your way of thinking.

John M Fisher, charter psychologist, change management and leadership development specialist

This book has helped me to understand why I feel the way I do when things change and has provided advice on how to handle it.

Cynthia Snyder, managing director of development and property management

An awesome book! With short sections that make sense for the business person wanting to learn something new, it gives a new slant on resilience and what it all means.

Dexter Vardarni, life and executive coach

A real authority guide! The chapters are succinct and to the point, yet helpful and practical. I have learned loads on resilience and managing stress that I didn't know before.

Berylla Gruber, business development executive

THE AUTHORITY GUIDE TO
EMOTIONAL RESILIENCE
IN BUSINESS

Second Edition

Strategies to manage stress and weather storms in the workplace

ROBIN HILLS

The Authority Guide to Emotional Resilience in Business

Strategies to manage stress and weather storms in the workplace

Second edition

© Robin Hills

ISBN 978-1-915483-86-7

eISBN 978-1-915483-87-4

Published in 2025 by Authority Guides

In the intervening period between writing the first edition of this book in 2016 and the second edition eight years later, the world has undergone much change. We have lived through a devastating pandemic; wars, shifting global powers and political turmoil have intensified; climate change continues apace, leading to extreme weather patterns; social media has proliferated and infiltrated our lives in many ways; and there has been the rise of artificial intelligence.

The world is constantly evolving, and these trends are likely to continue to shape the future. With this backdrop, we are striving to do the best for ourselves and our families to lead normal lives and to be resilient.

This second edition seeks to build upon the success of the first edition, bringing into focus different, newer perspectives around emotional resilience. I will admit to using AI systems to help me to construct this edition. These weren't available when the first one was written. They have been invaluable in ensuring my writing is concise, precise and readable. However, I must stress that these systems are limited by a lack of human experience and emotional understanding. This means some of the concepts presented in the book are beyond AI's abilities to expand upon the ideas in a meaningful way. Also, I disagree with some of the inherent biases within these tools.

Contents

Introduction

The strongest oak of the forest is not the one that is protected from the storm and hidden from the sun, but it is the one that stands in the open, where it's compelled to struggle for its existence against the winds and rains and the scorching sun.

Napoleon Hill, *The Law of Success* (1928)

How do your challenges inside and outside work impact upon your emotions and your resilience? The emotional resilience of those involved in a business will contribute significantly to the organisation's success.

Are you worn out from dealing with reduced resources, conflicting demands and relentless change? If you're angry, how do you react?

Are you controlled and rational, or do you say the first thing that comes to mind?

How do you react to pressure?

How do you manage stressful situations?

How do you manage your emotional responses to events?

How do others influence the way that you react to certain situations?

How do you cope as you sink in the quicksand of modern life filled with televisions and phones and social media and shopping and emails and advertisements and noise and traffic and the internet and remembering what it is that you may have forgotten?

Are you working with others who are struggling to maintain their own resilience?

Have you ever wondered why some people appear to remain calm in the face of disaster while others fail to cope?

People who are able to handle themselves well and remain calm in a crisis have what psychologists call resilience, an ability to cope with problems and setbacks.

Resilient people are able to utilise their capabilities, strengths and robustness to manage and recover from problems and challenges, and these may include job loss, financial problems, illness, medical emergencies, natural disasters, divorce or the death of a loved one.

People with resilience are able to adapt to adversity and major change without lasting difficulties, and generally they do this in a calm, rational manner.

Those who lack resilience may instead be overwhelmed by these experiences and have a much harder time with stress and life changes, both major and minor.

They may dwell on problems and use unhealthy coping mechanisms to deal with such challenges. Generally, these individuals recover from setbacks more slowly and may experience more psychological distress as a result.

Those capable of dealing with minor stresses more readily have been shown to manage major crises with greater ease

– so resilience has its benefits for daily life as well as for the rare major catastrophe.

How this book will help you

This book is crammed with insights and practical tips. It informs about ways to:

- change the way you think about yourself and how you approach situations
- move forward and develop your resilience at your own pace.

Treat the book as a practical manual and begin applying the tips before you've reached the end.

Just by reading the book, you can develop a greater understanding about resilience, but this won't change your levels of resilience. You need to go away and put into practice what you've learned.

What is resilience?

Material science defines resilience as the capability of a strained body to recover its size and shape after being subjected to adversity or stress.

Resilience, in psychology, is the ability to keep your cool and stay calm, to recover from or adjust easily to misfortune or change. In some cases, it's the ability to triumph in the face of adversity, to display tenacity, but not at the expense of reason.

Resilient people know that they're going to experience failure on occasion. They see it not as something to dwell on, but as an opportunity to move forward and accept that failure is a part of life.

To some degree, emotional and physical resilience are inborn abilities. Some people, by their nature, are less upset by changes and surprises. This can be observed in infancy and tends to be stable throughout their lives (Rutter 1993). Emotional resilience is also related to some factors that aren't under your control, such as age, gender and exposure to trauma.

However, resilience can be developed with a little effort if you know what to do. You can become more resilient, even if you're naturally more sensitive to life's difficulties.

Why resilience is useful

Everyone is working with greater uncertainty, ambiguity and change. Resilience helps employees and leaders to improve their effectiveness and sustain their efforts.

Resilience is about rationality and calmness, dealing effectively with – and making the most of – what you experience in everyday life.

Resilience enables you to:

- overcome misfortune
- steer through everyday challenges
- pick yourself up and move on when events take you off course
- reach out to new experiences and challenges that help you to achieve your full potential.

Developing a greater level of resilience won't stop bad or stressful things from happening but can reduce the level of disruption that stress can have and the time taken to recover.

When resilience is useful

Resilience is useful in situations that involve:

- rapid changes
- pressure to achieve more with less resources
- performing multiple tasks or roles
- loss of control
- greater workplace diversity
- outsourcing or downsizing
- balancing issues inside and outside work
- uncertainty about the future.

Resilience helps you to improve your effectiveness and sustain your efforts. Resilience is about rationality and calmness, dealing effectively with and making the most of what you experience in everyday life.

Being more resilient helps you to:

- retain a focus on what matters and supports effective behaviour
- increase your happiness in work and home life
- reduce your chances of succumbing to illness
- experience better psychological wellbeing and health
- increase your life expectancy.

So, developing resilience has a lot of benefits.

Individual resilience incorporates your physical health as well as your emotional and mental health and your wellbeing. All of these contribute to enabling you to adapt to different forms of adversity – frequently characterised as an inner strength, fortitude or heartiness, often termed 'grit'.

Developing resilience

Resilience is a mechanism that helps you to survive through adversity and recover from even the most hostile of situations.

While there are some genetic factors, resilience can be learned.

People who show good levels of resilience possess three distinct qualities:

- A firm, reliable acceptance of reality.
- A deep belief, supported by strongly held values, that life is meaningful.
- An ability to be creative, adaptable and to improvise.

Recovery from adverse situations is possible with one or two of these qualities, but to be truly resilient, you need to develop all three.

Resilience versus coping

Everyone must cope with the stresses and strains of everyday life. Challenges and changes are constant. Some of these involve taking some degree of risk, while some may be crises or emergencies that demand your immediate attention.

Adverse situations may be familiar or unfamiliar to you, depending upon whether you've experienced them before or whether you've experienced circumstances that may be similar. You will have developed coping mechanisms, and these will help you in dealing with familiar adverse situations and many unfamiliar ones.

Your self-talk (your inner voice) that you use in these situations will drive your thinking and your feelings leading to the decisions that you make and your subsequent actions and behaviours. Your emotional intelligence is a function of how you combine your thinking with your feelings to make good, authentic decisions and consequently how you act and behave.

All of these will add to your life experiences and will underpin your resilience.

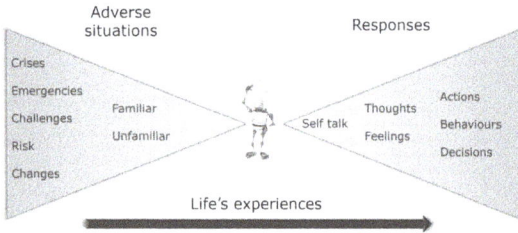

Figure 1: The stresses and strains of everyday life (our experience of adverse events drives our responses and reactions).

Reactions to adversity and stress

Coping is adapting your thinking and behaviour to manage demands that exceed the resources available to you or demands that you find taxing.

Resilience is the ability to recover from or adjust easily to misfortune or change. Resilience is an internal drive that relates critically to how you calmly engage with your environment.

Figure 2: How environment and behaviour influence each other.

So being resilient is more than just coping. It's about learning through the experience to grow personally and to become stronger and to deal with adversity better as you encounter it.

Your resilience is tied up in the interactions between your behaviour and your environment.

You can't control your environment, so your environment impacts upon you in a way that drives your reaction and the way that you behave.

Resilience is about finding meaning in your environment and using your core values to interpret and shape events.

For example, starting your day with an argument at home can leave you feeling annoyed, flustered and behind schedule. You leave for work only to be delayed on your commute. Add in a mountain of emails, including an urgent one that you had overlooked and an important meeting that you miss the start of, and the pressure can be immense. The way you manage your emotions in such a situation – staying focused or letting stress impact your judgement – will influence the atmosphere around you at work. If you choose to take your frustration out on your work colleagues, they're likely to react in ways that will increase your annoyance and cause you further problems. This will be even worse if you take out your frustrations on demanding customers or clients.

When stress takes over

Your resilience is affected by the way that you react to stressful situations.

Different people react to different situations in different ways. Your reaction will be affected by factors both inside and outside work. Your way of responding will be influenced by how you've coped with similar situations in the past and how successful you were in managing your stress and anxiety at that time. It will also be influenced by your personality.

When you're able to cope, you:

- are able to be flexible and adaptable
- are able to play to your strengths
- have a healthy outlook that is normal for you.

When stressed, you:

- start to lose your perspective
- feel that you're losing control
- react in exaggerated and immature ways.

When under extreme stress, you:

- become irrational
- act out of character
- lose control.

However, what you find stressful today may not necessarily be stressful to you tomorrow or the day after.

Resilience is more than coping

Coping is about putting up with the day-to-day stuff that leads to anxiety.

You can build and improve your ability to remain calm, to focus on what is important and to be resilient when faced with stressful and difficult situations.

You can learn to cope better by:

- seeking out new, meaningful and challenging experiences
- retaining realistic optimism and a sense of humour under stress

- adapting and improvising through your learning.
- not allowing your anxiety and doubts to become overwhelming
- viewing problems and challenges as opportunities
- aiming to succeed despite hardships
- learning from your mistakes or failures
- transforming your helplessness into power
- trying not to feel too ashamed or depressed in the face of failure
- moving from being a victim to being a survivor.

We'll explore some action strategies later on in the book with some hints and tips on how you can work to develop your resilience.

The role of risk in resilience

Taking risks is important in developing resilience, and this is going to be affected by your attitude towards risk.

Taking risks is going to be influenced by your fear of not doing the right thing or getting something wrong. When you don't take risks, you end up trying to cope.

It's important for you to identify emerging risks and to plan ways to manage these. You can develop strategies for managing emerging risks.

What's the worst that could happen, and what would you do to manage this if it does?

Identify what it is that drives your management of risk. Is it driven by financial concerns, or your concern for your reputation, or how it impacts upon your ethics and values? What do you need to make the decisions that are important to you?

Answering these questions will depend upon you: your attitudes, your personality and what information you have.

Once you're clear about the risks you face, you will need to be confident that your processes for managing them are effective. Your approach to managing risk should become embedded in your everyday working practices and applied consistently.

Working with too little or too much challenge

Challenge is healthy and life enhancing. Threat *can* be exciting. Some pressure stretches you, helps you to perform well and helps you to grow and develop.

The Yerkes–Dodson law describes the relationship between arousal and performance, showing that optimal performance occurs at moderate levels of arousal. The law was originally proposed by Robert M. Yerkes and John Dillingham Dodson in 1908. Since then, it has become widely known and is often referenced. The law suggests that performance improves with the increasing arousal that comes from moderate levels of stress, but only up to a certain point. Beyond the optimal point, performance begins to decline dramatically as excessive arousal can lead to anxiety, increased stress and decreased focus (see Figure 3). Performance peaks under the heightened activation that comes with moderate levels of stress. However, when levels of arousal or pressure become too high, performance decreases dramatically.

The first part of the curve shows that lack of challenge can be demotivating and can cause stress in its own way. Over time, this lack of challenge leads to frustration and boredom.

Your brain is wired so that it's difficult to take action until you feel at least some level of the emotional state and anxiety that's associated with stress. As long as the stress isn't prolonged, it's harmless. In the middle part of the curve, challenging, tough experiences can build high resilience, but only if the challenge seems worth it. Like an elastic band, you need some stretch to work at an optimal level. An elastic band doesn't work unless it's stretched. Too little and it won't function properly. Too much, and it becomes overstretched and will snap.

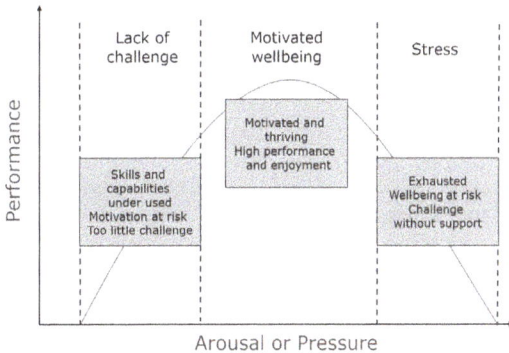

Figure 3: The impact of pressure on performance.

Chronic, uncontrollable pressure leads to constant stress, ultimately causing burnout. This manifests as exhaustion, lack of motivation and feelings of ineffectiveness, often accompanied by frustration or cynicism. The result of this heightened state of arousal is reduced performance that has a negative impact on workplace efficacy.

So, exposure to some degree of pressure, managed well and with suitable respite and support, leads to personal growth and builds resilience.

Building resilience beyond your comfort zone

Your comfort zone (Figure 4) is a behavioural state where you operate using a limited set of behaviours to deliver a steady level of performance. Within your comfort zone, you are able to cope. You experience little or no anxiety as you are not exposed to any risks, which provides a sense of security.

If you spend too much time within your comfort zone, you can become complacent – not really interested in what's going on around you and coasting through life, almost oblivious to what's happening as things change.

Figure 4: Learning and growth take place beyond your comfort zone, but don't push yourself too far, to avoid panic.

Step outside your comfort zone and you must experiment with new and different responses that enable you to endure within this environment. These responses will stretch you to experience new and different behaviours, enabling you to develop and grow.

Step too far away from your comfort zone and you're going to start to panic.

The fallacy of work–life balance

The term *work–life balance* has become a universal part of our modern work culture vocabulary. It's often presented as the ideal state of equilibrium, where personal and professional lives coexist harmoniously. It's used quite glibly without even thinking about the impact that this phrase has on other people. You probably even use the phrase yourself quite often.

However, as we delve deeper into the complexities of resilience, work and life, the phrase itself may be contributing to some of the problems it aims to solve.

The phrase 'work–life balance' inherently suggests a separation between work and life as if they exist in two separate compartments. This distinction can inadvertently create a mindset where work is seen as something to escape from, rather than being an integral part of life. It implies that work is a burden to be balanced against the rest of our existence, which can lead to negative perceptions of work itself.

In the age of remote work, gig economies and flexible schedules, the traditional boundaries between work and personal life are blurring. People may find themselves working from home outside regular hours or while on vacation. This changing landscape challenges the traditional concept of balance and calls for a more adaptive approach.

The term *balance* implies that both work and personal life should receive equal attention and energy, which can set unrealistic expectations. In reality, there are times when work demands may be higher, such as working towards an important deadline, working late, at weekends, working away from home, and there are other times when personal life takes precedence: holidays, family events such as weddings or birthday celebrations, health considerations such as sickness, visits to the doctor, the optician, the dentist and hospital appointments. Striving for a perfect balance at all times can lead to stress and guilt when this is unattainable.

Everybody's needs and preferences are unique, and what constitutes a healthy balance for one person will be different for another. Some may thrive on a busy work schedule, while others require more personal time. Using a one-size-fits-all term like 'work–life balance' fails to account for this diversity, making it difficult to address individual needs effectively.

Rather than aiming for a rigid balance, you will benefit from pursuing harmony between your work and your personal life that is appropriate for you as an individual. This means integrating work into your life in a way that aligns with your personal values and priorities. It's about making conscious choices and embracing the ebb and flow of different life phases.

While the phrase 'work–life balance' has good intentions, it often inadvertently perpetuates some of the challenges it seeks to address, hindering your ability to build resilience. Shift your perspective to focus on a harmonious integration of work as a part of life. Prioritise what is important and matters as this changes over time, and you'll navigate challenges with resilience, finding solutions that work for you.

Ultimately, it's about finding out what works best for you and crafting your life that reflects your values and aspirations.

The role of emotions in resilience

Emotions are mental and physiological states associated with a wide variety of feelings, thoughts and behaviours. Emotions blend together and are in continual flux. When you feel good about yourself, you feel optimistic and work better, with predictable results for creativity, personal relationships and profitability in all your achievements.

The way you feel is influenced by the emotions of people around you. Pleasant moods are the most contagious. Depression is not as contagious, but irritability and bad moods can influence others' feelings.

Far from being purely reactive, emotions are intricately linked to rational thinking, fuelling cognitive abilities, which include decision making, problem solving and creativity.

Emotions act as powerful signals that urge you to take action and guide your decisions. They trigger physiological changes within you and can even influence how others perceive your motivations.

Emotions play a crucial role in learning, helping you focus your attention and process information effectively.

The misconception about positive and negative emotions

There is an extremely popular misconception about emotions being either positive (good) or negative (bad), where positive emotions are seen as desirable and negative emotions as undesirable.

So-called *negative* emotions such as sadness can be a signal of loss, which can motivate self-reflection, prompting you to seek support, leading to creativity or encouraging you to make changes. Meanwhile *positive* emotions like elation may lead to risky behaviours and can have a negative impact on your ability to communicate effectively.

Emotions are complex and often multifaceted, yet they serve as valuable signals providing data about what is going on around you so that you can respond in the best way to survive and maximise your potential.

Emotions are psychological and physiological reactions to your environment. They alert you to potential problems or unmet needs. Ignoring them can hinder your ability to address challenges effectively.

This misconception about positive and negative emotions hinders the development of your emotional intelligence, limiting your ability to understand and manage the full spectrum of human emotions effectively. This will impact upon your ability to develop healthy connections with your emotions. It's important to recognise all emotions as valid and to learn how to manage them constructively.

The duality of emotions

Emotions can be experienced as unpleasant or pleasant and can be constructive forces in your life, motivating positive actions and helping you to navigate challenges. However, the key lies in understanding and managing them effectively as unchecked emotions can also lead you down destructive paths.

Pleasant emotions

Happiness is considered to be a pleasant emotion that promotes creativity, supports connection with others and motivates people to pursue goals. Yet, unchecked, happiness can lead to destructive behaviours such as underestimating hazards or ignoring potential problems. For example, feeling overly happy about a business venture might lead to over-confidence, neglecting crucial planning steps and ultimately causing the venture to fail.

Another example is excitement. Excitement can propel you to try new things and embrace life's trials and tribulations. However, excessive excitement can cloud your judgement, leading to impulsive decisions or reckless behaviours. Think of someone getting swept away by the thrill of gambling and accumulating significant debt.

Unpleasant emotions

Unpleasant emotions often get a bad press, but they serve valuable purposes. Anger, for instance, can alert you to injustice and motivate you to stand up for yourself or others. However, uncontrolled anger can lead to aggression and damage relationships. Imagine someone lashing out at a colleague in a fit of rage, jeopardising their professional standing.

Fear, often identified as unpleasant and debilitating, can be a powerful emotion for self-preservation. It motivates you to avoid danger and take necessary precautions. However, excessive fear can cripple you, preventing you from taking healthy risks or pursuing opportunities. For example, someone overwhelmed by the fear of public speaking might miss out on making presentations, which could then limit their career opportunities.

The key to harnessing the power of emotions in resilience lies in understanding the information that they contain and consequently managing them effectively. Recognising the potential downsides and destructive behaviours of both pleasant and unpleasant emotions enables you to channel them constructively.

The neuroscience of resilience

The prefrontal cortex is implicated in planning complex cognitive behaviour, expressing personality, decision making and in moderating social behaviour. Resilience is marked by more activity in the left prefrontal cortex, which is associated more specifically with memory. The amount of activity in the left prefrontal region could be 30 times greater in a resilient person than in someone who is not (Davidson 2004).

The amygdalae are a pair of almond-shaped sets of neurons located deep in the brain's medial temporal lobe forming part of the limbic system, the emotional part of the brain. There is one in each hemisphere, and they play a key role in processing and filtering of emotions.

There are large bundles of neurons running between certain regions of the prefrontal cortex and each amygdala, effectively creating communication pathways. In more resilient people, it's been shown by fMRI scanning that they have more white matter (axons that connect one neuron to another) between the prefrontal cortex and the amygdalae (Kim & Whalen 2009).

People with greater activation of the prefrontal cortex recover quickly from strong feelings and emotions. Inhibitory signals are quickly sent to the amygdalae to lower their activity. This enables the brain to recuperate from an experience and so these people recover more rapidly from adverse, upsetting situations.

Interestingly, highly resilient people may exhibit a calmer amygdala response. While this can be positive for managing stress, it could also influence their ability to empathise and fully connect with the emotions of others.

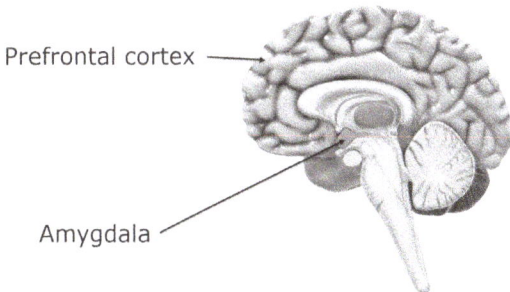

Prefrontal cortex

Amygdala

Figure 5: Diagram of the brain showing the location of the prefrontal cortex and amygdala.

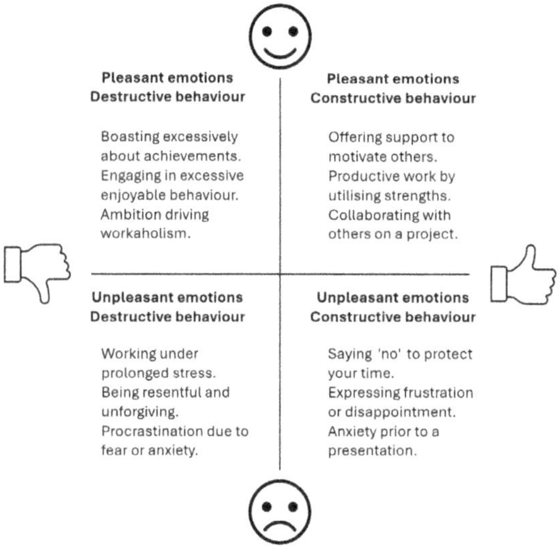

Pleasant emotions
Destructive behaviour

Boasting excessively
about achievements.
Engaging in excessive
enjoyable behaviour.
Ambition driving
workaholism.

Pleasant emotions
Constructive behaviour

Offering support to
motivate others.
Productive work by
utilising strengths.
Collaborating with
others on a project.

Unpleasant emotions
Destructive behaviour

Working under
prolonged stress.
Being resentful and
unforgiving.
Procrastination due to
fear or anxiety.

Unpleasant emotions
Constructive behaviour

Saying 'no' to protect
your time.
Expressing frustration
or disappointment.
Anxiety prior to a
presentation.

Figure 6: Pleasant and unpleasant emotions with some examples of constructive and destructive behaviours.

Emotions that drain or impair resilience

Certain emotions in stressful situations can drain or impair the development of resilience. Here are a few of the most common emotions with an example of a thought pattern and an example of a specific thought.

Your emotion	Example of a thought pattern	Example of a specific thought
Discomfort	Uncertain of capabilities	Am I able to continue doing this?
Fear	Uncertainty of outcomes	I am not sure what is going on or what is going to happen
Hurt	Values have been exposed and ignored	My best efforts have not been recognised
Anger	Violation of my rights	I deserve more credit or support
Frustration	Lack of resources	There's nothing more I can do
Disappointment	Standards have not been met	Others are not doing what I expect of them
Anxiety	Future threat	Work or my relationships are going to suffer
Guilt	Violation of other's rights	My family deserve better than this
Embarrassment	Loss of face/ inadequacy	People can see I can't manage
Hopelessness	Unable to cope	I can't go on with things as they are
Loneliness	No one else cares	I'm on my own with this

Emotions that enhance or facilitate resilience

Certain emotions in stressful situations can facilitate or enhance the development of resilience. Here are a few of the most common emotions with an example of a thought pattern and an example of a specific thought.

Your emotion	Example of a thought pattern	Example of a specific thought
Happiness	Things are going well	I can be more creative and push the limits
Pride	I am performing admirably or well	The team need me to help them achieve
Contentment	My needs are satisfied	Life is good
Engagement	Here is a challenge I am fully involved in	More information will develop me and the situation
Esteem	People think well of me	I will enjoy, explore and share experiences
Love	I feel connected with and committed to others	I am confident in taking on new challenges
Excitement	I feel energised by the challenge ahead	I want to do whatever I can
Optimism	Things will work out whatever happens	My contribution is a key part of our success
Enthusiasm	This is absorbing and interesting	I have the energy to give whatever I can
Passion	I am compelled to devote myself	I am earnestly dedicated to what we are doing

Emotions alert you to challenges and motivate you to take action. While strong emotions during tough times are normal, effective resilience involves managing these emotions – not ignoring them. By understanding your emotional responses, you can make realistic decisions and approach challenges with a healthy perspective, ultimately strengthening your ability to learn and grow through difficult times.

Managing emotions

Before considering anyone else's emotions, it's important to be aware of your own.

It's crucial that you're able to understand and manage your own emotions so that you don't behave in ways that have a negative impact on others around you.

Managing your emotions doesn't mean denying your feelings or putting on a false front – it's about behaving in such a way that your emotions don't cause damage to your relationships and to other people.

Emotions are expressed in your body language, your voice, your tone and your behaviour, so it's essential to be aware of how you come across to others and the impact that you have, determining what you need to do differently.

People will need to feel that they can trust you and rely on you, so you need to manage your thoughts, feelings and behaviours in order that you can remain calm, collected and objective.

To ensure that you understand and acknowledge other's emotions, you need to really listen in order to see and feel things from their perspective and experience how real it is for them.

Everyone's different. Things that you don't consider stressful or worrying may be really frightening for someone else.

Empathise without judgement and without criticism. The most effective change leaders are those who can navigate their own reservations while guiding others through the transformation process. You may be torn between how you're feeling and how others are feeling – especially if any anger or criticism is directed at you personally, which may lead you to experience high levels of stress.

By becoming aware of this, you can develop coping strategies to manage your levels of stress and so prioritise your health and wellbeing.

From setback to comeback

Change is the only constant.

Change can be stressful. It challenges your ability to cope and can drain your resilience.

When implementing change, organisations typically focus on the systems, processes and outcomes, often overlooking the emotional impact this will have on people. Equipping people both physically and emotionally to deal with change effectively will significantly develop the resilience of the individual, the team and the organisation.

To do this, it's important to:

- find out as much as possible about any impending changes or challenges
- understand the reasons for the changes and why they are happening
- determine what isn't changing
- acknowledge what it is that will be lost
- shift any negativity towards creativity, improvisation and problem solving

- break down issues, problems and challenges into small, bite-sized, manageable parts
- listen to people's anxieties and fears, which are very real to them
- engage others to develop a shared vision towards a realistic, optimistic future.
- maintain a healthy balance around work commitments, balancing these with commitments outside of work
- celebrate small victories.

Resilience in change

Change is all around us. The pace of change seems to be unrelenting. It appears to occur faster and faster with every year, month or even week that passes. How you respond to change can make all the difference to how resilient you are to it.

With the right approach and focus, change presents a valuable and exciting opportunity for organisations, management teams and especially the people who will implement it. Their success will be key in driving positive change as they will be the ones responsible for making change work.

Change brings about a new set of emotions that offer you the chance to authentically reconnect to who you truly are.

Coaching and empowering people through change are functions of effective leadership. You cannot overcommunicate in times of change.

The role of the leader in times of change is to:

- explain the change journey, to give it meaning and to show the way
- communicate (you cannot afford to avoid or ignore

delivering messages about change)
- understand the emotional impact that the change will have; to empathise and to care
- provide clarity when there is uncertainty
- challenge where appropriate
- empower people to bring about and effect the change.

How do you feel about the changes? Are you feeling completely comfortable and positive, or do you have concerns yourself? You may be fearful about your future and, despite this, you may find yourself taking a lot of blame and a lot of the criticism for the change. This might upset you and make you angry.

Working through a setback

- Accept the reality of the situation.
- Identify and deal with emotions.
- Consider the situation from a different perspective (this doesn't have to be true – just believe it!).
- Learn from the situation.
- Identify the benefits open to you.
- Identify the new skills you need and can develop.
- Consciously choose to let go – change what you can; let go of what you cannot.

The phases from setback to comeback

Everyone goes through a similar emotional pathway when dealing with significant change.

John M Fisher's Process of Transition curve (Figure 7) explains how people respond to change through defined phases that follow in succession until they accept the changes.

This change theory is based on earlier studies by Elisabeth Kûbler-Ross, who identified various stages of grief. John Fisher's model is a more focused approach to change in organisations and business.

Much of the transition through the phases is completed subconsciously. Change happens at different paces for different people. People have unique approaches to change and different needs, which are influenced by the phase that they are in.

Other factors that have an influence are their temperament, their attitude, their life experiences, their perceived degree of control, whatever else is going on in their life at the time, and so on.

The key to understanding the phases is not to feel that you must go through every one of them in precise order. Some people may regress to an earlier stage depending upon their circumstances. Instead, it's more helpful to consider each of the phases as guides as people transition through the change process. The phases help you to put into context and to understand where you and others are emotionally.

Keep in mind that everyone reacts differently. Some people will readily show their emotions, while others will experience their emotions more internally, keeping them under control. You shouldn't try to judge how a person experiences change and how they respond emotionally as everybody will their own way of experiencing change.

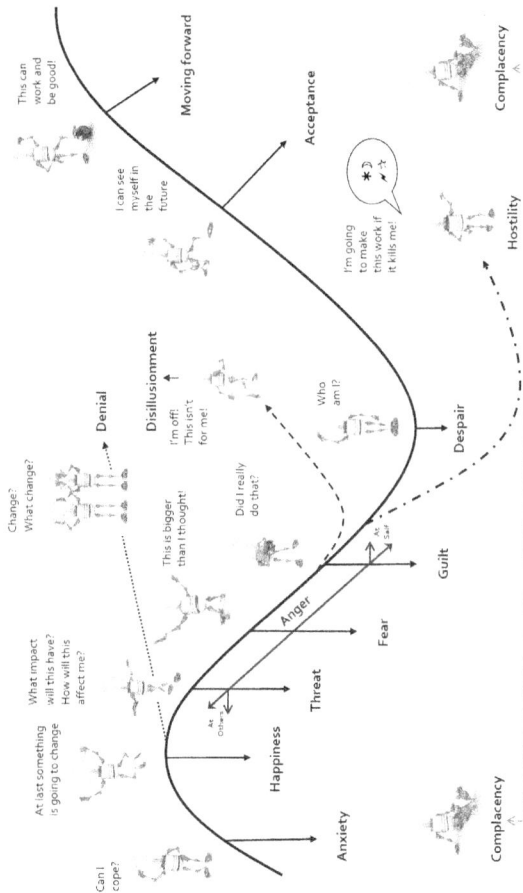

Figure 7: John Fisher's Personal Transition through Change Curve. Copies of the curve can be downloaded from EI4Change: ei4change.com/resources

Can I cope?

At the beginning of the change process, you don't have enough information that enables you to anticipate behaving in a different way within the new order. Anxiety is an awareness that events lie outside your understanding or control – you are unable to picture the future clearly.

There's a sense of disbelief around the change of circumstances, and some short-term denial may help to protect from strong emotions. You are unsure how you're going to cope with the new work and the new social situations.

Helping others deal with anxiety

- Listen and understand their sense of loss.
- Give them time to come to terms with the situation.
- Encourage them to ask questions when they're ready and give them all the information that is possible.
- Focus on short-term goals and short-term objectives.
- Give people any reassurance that they need.

Happiness

At last, something is going to change.

Happiness is an awareness that your viewpoint about the need for change has been recognised and is being shared by others. You have a feeling of relief that something's going to change and not continue as before. Whether the past is perceived positively or negatively, there is still a feeling of anticipation and maybe excitement at the possibility of some improvement.

There is some satisfaction that some of your thoughts about the old system were correct and that something is going to be done about it.

Helping others deal with happiness

- Learn from the mistakes that were made in the past.
- Help them to construct plans for the future that ensure mistakes in the system are not repeated.
- Encourage them to support others who may not be feeling as they do.

Denial

Change? What change?

It takes time to face up to the change and its repercussions, so don't expect any sudden leaps into acceptance. This phase is defined by a lack of acceptance of any change. You deny that it's going on or that it's impacting you in any way. You continue to act as if the change is not happening, using old practices and processes, and ignoring evidence or information to the contrary. Without the right level of support, you can easily get stuck in this phase.

Helping others deal with denial

- Give them sufficient time to face up to the change.
- Explain carefully, and sensitively, the risks of staying in denial.
- Explain carefully, and sensitively, the impact that their denial will have on them individually, and how this is going to affect you, the team and the organisation.

Anger

Who's at fault? Me or you?

Initially, some frustration is directed at others to apportion blame. This anger is directed at anyone and everyone else through *threats and fear* and is especially focused on those you believe are responsible for the change. Part of the expression of anger is to bargain – to try to return things to how they were before. There is the threat of having to change yourself and your perception of who you are.

You blame others for this situation and for causing you stress.

Eventually, your anger and frustration are directed internally at yourself as you come to terms with the change, and will be combined with feelings of guilt for not having coped as well as you believe that you should have. You become angry at yourself for not knowing better and allowing the situation to escalate outside your control.

Helping others deal with anger

Any anger directed at you may be unpleasant or upsetting. It's important to avoid taking comments personally or reacting defensively. Instead, focus on understanding the underlying issue and responding calmly and professionally.

- Keep channels of communication open.
- Be honest and don't try to hide from the truth.
- Don't make promises that can't be kept.
- Help others to understand the limits of the change and what's not changing.
- Help to guide them so that they feel that they have some control.

Disillusionment

I'm off! This isn't for me!

When a mismatch arises between your personal values, beliefs and goals and those of your organisation, disillusionment sets in. This disconnect can lead to a sharp decline in motivation and focus. Dissatisfaction grows, and you might find yourself withdrawing mentally or physically. Mentally, this could manifest as going through the motions, doing only the bare minimum, or even actively undermining change through criticism or complaints. Physically, it could lead to resignation. Without the right level of support, you can easily get stuck in this phase.

Helping others deal with disillusionment

- Encourage them to talk about their feelings.
- Be honest and don't try to hide from the truth.
- Don't make promises that can't be kept.
- Help them to understand the limits of the change and what is not changing.
- Help to guide them, so they feel they have some control.
- Explain carefully and sensitively the impact that their disillusionment will have on them individually, and how this will affect you, the team and the organisation.
- If they have made the decision to leave the organisation, give them as much help and support as possible.

Hostility

I'm going to make this work if it kills me!

Anger and frustration may lead you to become more hostile. The problem here is that you continue to operate some of the processes that are no longer part of the new system and have repeatedly failed to achieve a successful outcome or are surplus to the new ways of working. The new processes are ignored at best or actively undermined at worst. You can get stuck in this phase, yet you will appear to have moved on and to be accepting the new order.

Helping others deal with hostility

- Encourage them to talk about their feelings.
- Help to guide them so that they feel they have some control.
- Explain carefully, and sensitively, the impact that their hostility will have on them individually and how this is going to affect them, the team and the organisation.

Depression or despair

Who am I?

This is the most difficult phase to work through and could last the longest of all the phases. It is characterised by confusion and lack of motivation, combined with feelings of sadness, apathy and hopelessness. You are uncertain as to what the future holds and how you fit into the new future world. You may feel a deep loss of the things that were important to you and feel completely powerless. You may struggle with your focus, your work and dealing with others. The undermining of who you think you are leaves you adrift with no sense of identity and no clear vision of how to operate.

Helping others deal with despair

- Encourage them to talk about their feelings.
- Identify sources of support.
- Help them to find ways to manage their feelings and thinking patterns.

- If necessary, and the feelings of despair evolve into clinical depression, it's important to encourage them to seek professional help.

Acceptance

I can see myself in the future.

During the acceptance phase, you find that you have become more emotionally detached from the situation. You begin to make sense of your circumstances and of your place within the change. Your confidence is returning as you are regaining some control over the change process and you are having some meaningful success. You begin to put new plans in place and formulate goals around your new needs and wishes. You feel good as you are doing the right things in the right way.

Helping others deal with acceptance

- Recognise and reward them for the progress that they are making.
- Provide them with positive, supportive feedback.
- Give people something to feel proud of.
- Continue to give them a positive vision of the future.

Moving forward

This can work and can be good!

In this final phase, you exert more control and make things happen in a positive sense. You get back your old sense of self. You know who you are once more and feel comfortable that you are acting in line with your convictions, beliefs and so on, and that you are making the right choices. Within this phase, you experiment again more actively and effectively within your environment.

Helping others deal with moving forward

- Continue to keep communication channels open.
- Provide positive support and encouragement.
- Look at building resilient teams (see page 67).
- Consider ways of mapping minds (thinking processes) and mapping hearts (emotional engagement) (see pages 73–4) to confirm that the changes have been in everyone's best interest.

Ensure that everyone remains emotionally aligned and continue to affect the changes with appropriate support for others.

Complacency

There is also a further stage of complacency, which forms the initial stage and the final stage of the change curve. Here you have survived the change, rationalised the events, incorporated them into your new ways of thinking and behaving and have come to terms with the new reality.

This is where you feel that you have, once again, moved back into your comfort zone and believe that you won't encounter anything further that is either outside your world view or that can't be incorporated into it with ease. You know the right decisions to make and can predict future events with a high degree of certainty.

Complacency means that you are subsequently laid back and coasting through the job, not focused too much on events that shape your environment. You are operating well within your comfort zone. In some respects, you have forgotten about, or are now oblivious to, what happened as you transitioned through the change process, even though it may have been quite traumatic at the time.

Looking after yourself

During periods of change and uncertainty, it's essential to look after yourself and encourage others to look after themselves as well.

In order to work effectively with change, you need to be mentally tough and resilient. You also need to be physically healthy.

To maintain your health:

- Eat a balanced diet of foods rich in nutrients like vitamins, minerals, fibre and healthy fats.
- Drink plenty of fluids.
- Limit your caffeine and alcohol intake.
- Exercise regularly.
- Get the right amount of sleep.
- Take breaks and holidays.
- Use relaxation techniques that work for you.
- Seek support from family, friends and colleagues.

The characteristics of resilient people

Resilience is a metaphor

The word 'resilience' is widely used in everyday language. It can be applied to people, it can be applied to teams, it can be applied to organisations. However, resilience has different meanings in different contexts.

In fact, *resilience* is a *metaphor*.

A metaphor is a figure of speech that describes the subject by comparing it to, and describing it in terms of, an otherwise-unrelated topic.

- Metaphors can represent experiences more fully as an abstract concept and so enable more effective communication.
- Metaphors condense information, making things more tangible and easier to work with.
- The metaphor for an experience has a similar structure to the experience that it represents

The idea of resilience is particularly common in material science, where it describes the ability of a material to return to its original state from deformation or stress on release of the pressure.

However, the concept of resilience goes beyond this physical property. It has been adopted and adapted to describe a similar characteristic in living things and even abstract systems.

In the context of human psychology, resilience as a metaphor and behaviour works, but the metaphor from material science has serious limitations.

What about too much resilience?

What about learning, growing and developing through stress?

What about adapting to situations and environments?

In all these scenarios, the metaphor doesn't work so well.

Why resilience is contextual

How would you react to a natural disaster, an aircraft crash, a terrorist attack, being caught up in a civil uprising, being taken hostage, losing a limb, the death of a loved one in unusual circumstances, financial ruin and so on? How calm would you be?

Fortunately, it's statistically unlikely that you will experience any of these situations. But what if you did? Your reaction may surprise you. You may remain calm and respond well or you may react in a way that will cause you anxiety over time.

The intensity of the situation and the strength of your emotions will cause you to react in one of the following ways:

- freeze, where you're unable to take any action at all
- show a fight response – aggressively facing the situation head on
- show a flight response – get away from the situation as quickly as possible

- react with an appropriate set of behaviours to deal with the circumstances.

You will not know how you are going to react until you experience this extreme adversity. And how you react on one occasion will not necessarily determine how you respond if you're faced with another adverse situation.

Underpinning your resilience will be your ability to accept the reality of the situation and its meaning to you. Your conscious decision making will be underpinned by a strong sense of core values that enable you to use your flexibility and creativity to improvise in a way that will see you through to a suitable end point.

Increasing levels of resilience

At one extreme, people are so beaten down by adversity that they are extremely slow to recover or they don't recover at all. At the other extreme, people recover quickly from adversity and shrug off any setbacks.

In between, there are increasing levels of resilience. With changes in the environment, your resilience capacity changes.

In normal functioning, you either react negatively to circumstances that cause disruption in your life and your resilience capacity is lowered or you react more positively, and you adapt to changing situations. You grow through the experience, thus increasing your resilience capacity (adaptation).

New levels of resilience occur through major change whereby you transform your resilience capacity through absorbing the learning that you gain from the experience (transformation).

There's yet another level of resilience, where a person transforms an extreme challenge into an opportunity and achieves good outcomes from the setback even in the face of extreme loss through absorption.

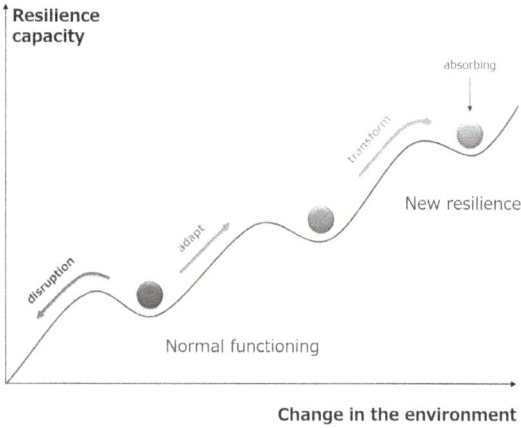

Figure 8: How your resilience capacity changes as your environment changes.

Constructing resilience

In human psychology, resilience takes on a more meaningful definition by considering these three key characteristics:

- An ability to accept harsh reality – assessing the situation objectively, setting aside personal opinions and biases, separating emotions and personal experiences and without denial.
- An ability to find meaning in adversity – to build bridges from an ordeal in the present to a fuller, better future.

- An ability to continually improvise – putting resources to unfamiliar uses and imagining possibilities that others can't see.

Fortunately, all of these characteristics that make up resilience can be developed.

Resilience is a mindset

Resilience is less about who you are and more about how you think.

As we've seen, the way that you think about a situation directly influences and shapes how you view the world and how you view yourself in the world. Your calmness, composure and, therefore, your resilience will be affected by your perception of the situation.

Some people have a more optimistic mindset than others and so are more naturally resilient.

Some people have a mindset that requires lower levels of perfection than others and so are more naturally resilient.

Your assumptions or attitudes influence your behaviours and the skills you develop. These behaviours and skills, in turn, influence your assumptions and attitudes so that a dynamic process is set up that continually operates – one which feeds on the other.

Behaviours, thoughts and actions can be learned and developed in anyone. It's not easy, but with work, patience, time and practice, you can train your mindset to be more resilient.

Your capacity to adapt requires an understanding of your perspective and your ability to grasp the context of the situation that you're in, requiring an ability to support yourself and to pace yourself.

Your capacity to adapt is a sophisticated mix of skills that connect your internal resources and your external goal focus and are in continuous motion.

Mastering a pacing cycle means constantly adjusting your workload to stay within your current capacity for optimal performance. These skills require:

- perspective – the ability to grasp context
- assessing your capacity and understanding your current energy levels, mental focus and ability to handle stress
- adjusting your load to match your workload to your current capacity – this could involve taking breaks, delegating tasks or scaling back your efforts temporarily
- monitoring your progress by regularly checking your energy levels and adjusting your workload as needed to maintain optimal performance.

It's about knowing when enough is enough and knowing how to refresh and energise yourself. Resilience becomes an advanced skill when you combine both learned skills and flexible behaviours to manage stress within your ever-evolving capacity to adapt to challenges.

The body's reaction to adversity

A change in your environment may be perceived as a threat or a challenge. In either situation, your body undergoes a range of biochemical and physiological changes, which are controlled by the autonomic nervous system and prepare you to take flight or to fight.

These changes include:

- an increase in your heart rate along with your blood pressure
- your muscles hardening and tensing in preparation for action
- your digestive system, not considered essential for immediate survival, slowing down through a reduced blood flow, and more acid being produced in the stomach to prepare for faster digestion if needed later
- your breathing becomes faster so that you can take in more oxygen and release more carbon dioxide.

This is known as the acute stress response. Your brain can't distinguish between a real or a potential threat, and so chronic exposure to the acute stress response leads to longer-term stress-related problems.

Prolonged stress can lead to not only physical issues, but also mental issues, both of which can reduce your ability to cope and your ability to deal with stress and will have a detrimental effect on your resilience.

Resilience involves managing your flight or fight reactions to real or imagined threats. These include:

- your perception of the event
- what is causing you stress (the stressor)
- your stress threshold
- what else causes you stress
- how you coped with the stressor in the past
- the level of control that you have over the stressor
- the duration of the stressor
- your values, your beliefs and your thinking style
- how sensitive you and your nervous system are at the time.

Being antifragile – the resilience of the future

Resilience defined by material science advocates that once the stress or strain is removed, the material returns to its unstressed state. It bounces back without any indication that it's been subjected to any stress.

This is a physical property of the material itself, often related to mechanical properties such as the elasticity and ductility evaluated on a relatively short timescale. Resilience in psychology involves complex psychological and emotional processes, including coping mechanisms, emotional regulation, problem-solving skills and social support networks. These are evaluated over longer timescales.

Research and publications by Professor Nassim Taleb, distinguished professor of risk engineering, have introduced the concept of antifragility (2012).

Antifragility suggests that certain systems (often seen within computing and engineering) can get better and improve when subjected to stress and strain. In other words, they're able to adjust to changing circumstances and so they can become more adapted to their environments.

As a human being, you evolve and improve yourself by learning from your accidents and mistakes and when you are subjected to adverse situations and, in this way, you develop your resilience. Like antifragile systems, you're able to self-adjust to dynamically changing circumstances and environments, to improve and to get better.

You're able to organise yourself in a proactive way so that you can determine your best strategies to become sustainable, to achieve high performance and to be energy efficient. You're able to personalise your attitudes and reactions in a way that's unique to you, and you can learn how to get better while doing it.

The metaphor of being antifragile should become increasingly recognised as having more relevance to resilience, particularly in the field of human psychology, over the coming years.

The behaviours
of resilient people

Perfectionism is a personality trait characterised by striving for flawlessness and setting excessively high standards of performance. This is often accompanied by being overly self-critical and may be combined with concerns about what other people may think.

Perfectionism can take three distinctive forms.

1 Self-oriented – you drive perfection in yourself and in everything that you do.

2 Other-oriented – you work towards perfection demanded of you by others.

3 Socially prescribed – you think others expect perfection-ism of you.

How you work with your level of perfectionism is going to impact upon and affect your resilience.

Perfectionism can drive people to accomplish their goals and provide the motivation to persevere in the face of discourage-ment and obstacles, and in this way can support resilience.

On the other hand, constant pressure to meet externally driven high standards, if other-oriented or socially-prescribed, is going to limit the development of resilience. Self-oriented perfectionism, which creates cognitive dissonance when you're unable to meet your own expectations, can lead to psychological and physiological issues that will also limit the development of resilience.

Ideally, perfectionism for resilience is a blend of intrinsic, self-oriented perfectionism held in check by extrinsic, other-oriented and socially prescribed perfectionism.

The role of optimism

The research by Professor Martin Seligman on optimism shows how emotional behaviours can lead to greater happiness and more success (2006).

Optimistic people are physically healthier and less prone to virtually every illness. Not surprisingly, they are markedly happier. In sports and in academia, optimists outperform pessimists who have similar levels of talent.

Optimism focuses upon how you explain your experiences in the world through three separate factors.

- Pervasiveness – do you generalise your response to an event or do you localise it?
- Permanence – do you think a particular event is permanent or is it temporary?
- Personal – do you take an event personally or impersonally? How much control do you have over the event?

The optimist relishes the good times and is unmoved by the bad.

The pessimist suffers the bad times and derives little pleasure from the good.

However, resilience needs more than pure optimism. Creating a sense of possibility can be very powerful, but it requires confronting a current reality that is not too distorted by rose-tinted spectacles. So, the true optimism of resilience will be tempered by a rational, practical pessimism of the situation.

Attitude to change

As we saw in the chapter 'From setback to comeback', change is constant and inevitable.

For some people, change brings overwhelming discomfort. This may be linked to fear: 'If the rules have changed, how can I continue to succeed?' Or it could be linked to a need to feel in control: 'If I don't do it my way, the way that I've always done it, then it won't be right.'

Some people try to deny change by focusing on the skills that have brought them success in the past and ignore what's required to adapt sooner or later. This lack of flexibility results in a mistake that has serious repercussions.

Successful people accept, change and adapt to it. They examine change on its own terms and they decide what they're in control of and what they can't control, so they know what to let go of. They move their energy away from any anxiety produced by change towards developing new skills and extending their current strengths.

How can you work better with change?

- Look for reasons to make the change work rather than why the change won't work.
- Make suggestions for increasing the effectiveness of the change.
- Show willingness to learn new methods, procedures, techniques or skills.
- Shift your priorities and your attitude to the demands of the situation.

How too much resilience causes problems

True resilience may be a balance between a rapid neurological response and a response to the depth of cognitive processing – how much awareness, perception, reasoning and judgement are used in assimilating information about circumstances.

Overly resilient people might become numb to problems or challenges, neglecting to address them proactively. This can lead to missed opportunities for improvement, ignoring others' concerns or prevent them from seeking help when truly needed.

By recovering and adapting to events too quickly, people can often appear to be too controlled and might unintentionally come across as unemotional or aloof. This can be especially true when others are still processing their own anxieties. While their resilience is a strength, it's important to acknowledge the emotions of those around them to avoid appearing insensitive.

Empathy is an asset towards surviving and thriving in any environment and consequently for developing resilience. It involves seeing things from other people's perspectives and viewpoints, and promotes a genuine curiosity, which facilitates the desire to learn and to understand. Understanding that people may have perceptions different from yours will ensure that other viewpoints are considered. By practising empathy, those with too much resilience can gain valuable insights into how their behaviour is seen by others, ensuring their resilience doesn't come at the cost of social awareness.

With empathy, anyone with too much resilience is unlikely to create problems through their behaviour. Such a person can assertively address situations yet take measures to ensure other's needs are taken into consideration and are respected.

Developing the ability to ask how others are coping, and to truly listen, ensures that their needs are accurately understood so that these are met and without any detrimental effects to the relationship. In this way, everyone becomes emotionally engaged and supported to adapt in their own time and in their own manner.

Techniques to address misunderstandings with others can usually be very effective; however, they only work if the person using the techniques is genuinely empathetic.

Mindfulness

You are not your thoughts. Your thoughts and feelings arise out of processing information unconsciously and combine with your physiology to create your reactions and your behaviours. You can take responsibility for your thoughts, feelings and behaviours and work on your own issues as an individual.

Buddhists have been meditating using mindfulness techniques for more than 2,000 years. Mindfulness has become increasingly popular in Western society in recent years and is seen as a fundamental behaviour for developing resilience.

Mindfulness is a form of meditation that encourages you to focus on your breathing – breathing out more slowly than you breathe in – and to acknowledge the fleeting nature of your thoughts. With mindfulness you live in the present – in the moment – physically and emotionally, to clear your mind of clutter about what you did in the past or what you're going to do in the future. By clearing your mind, you can focus on what's really important and what really matters. A disorderly way of thinking can lead to leaping mindlessly into your usual routine or interaction, which can reduce resilience.

Through mindfulness, you're able to become more consciously aware and more focused on your emotional and physical needs to ensure that you're not neglecting them. When you're mindful you can take control and are likely to enjoy more productive interactions with others.

How coaching helps

Coaching is a good intervention that can be used to support the development of resilience. Everyone's way of experiencing the world is different and using active listening and appropriate questioning techniques directs attention in some way.

Coaching prompts context, references and past experiences that are personal, making possible shifts in perspective, and an awareness that leads to insights which can support the growth of individual resilience. This awareness can lead to behaviour change and long-term learning, especially when supported by the right methods.

Working with too much resilience

Everyone has their own interpretation of reality. Everyone has a different purpose, a different set of values and different goals. So everyone's response to change and challenge is different.

Transitioning through challenges and change is very personal, impacted by various factors. What stresses one person might not faze another. This leads to diverse responses and, sometimes, conflicting strategies. These differences can create further challenges when managing change together.

Extreme resilience can lead to a mentality of being tough where vulnerability is seen as weakness and potentially disregarding others' struggles.

People who adapt too quickly might unintentionally appear insensitive to other's feelings. It's crucial to remember that everyone has a unique pace of adjustment. Demonstrating empathy and understanding these differences is key. By being supportive and respecting individual approaches, people can be encouraged to adapt in their own time. This approach fosters a positive environment for everyone to navigate change success-fully. Without it, rapid adaptation can be perceived as self-centred, leaving those struggling to adapt feeling unsupported.

It's worth noting that resilience is neither ethically good nor bad. Resilience is merely the skill and capability to be robust under conditions of stress and change. Values, whether positive or negative, are important for developing resilience. However, these could be considered to be self-serving or ruthless at times, depending upon your perspective. If you're working with someone with too much resilience, it's important to help them to understand through open communication and feedback to inform them how their actions and behaviours are detrimental to the development of resilience in others.

The poison in resilience

Resilience has become a ubiquitous term, such that the overuse and misuse of the words *resilient* and *resilience* can be misleading. Countless news bulletins and documentaries about recent events and even sporting commentaries are liberally littered with the words.

The focus on individual resilience can detract from addressing the root causes of hardship, especially for marginalised groups facing systemic inequality. This goes along with the capacity and compliance to accept less than favourable circumstances that may include inadequate resourcing, inequitable conditions and political agendas that work against people's long-term wellbeing. It is important to watch for the poison in resilience when marginalised people, including ethnic minorities, disabled, gender fluid or neurodiverse people among others, are labelled as resilient as this can have other implications.

There is the need to consider the circumstances that enable someone to overcome adversity. Support systems and fair treatment play a crucial role. Labelling someone as being resilient shouldn't be an excuse for shifting responsibility or inaction.

The terms *resilient* and *resilience* used within their correct context avoid trivialising both the challenges faced and the strength required to overcome adversity. Acknowledging the complexities of resilience involves accepting that at times it's okay not to be okay, whereby resilience can be used to support growth and positive change, not a justification for inaction or the normalisation of hardship.

Team resilience

Resilient teams

A team is considered to be resilient when the sources of pressure are well managed and there are high levels of individual wellbeing so that overall performance benefits.

Team resilience goes beyond individual strength. It's the collective ability of the individuals working together in the team to adjust and work around the challenges they face, adapt to change and maintain focus on goals even in the face of adversity. It involves strong communication, mutual support and shared trust within the team, enabling them to navigate difficulties together and emerge even stronger.

Distinct predictors of team outcomes are seen in the levels of cohesion, cooperation, coordination, conflict and team satisfaction. There's team optimism. The individuals in the team look out for each other to ensure there are high levels of psychological wellbeing across the whole team, avoiding burnout and ensuring sustainable levels of performance.

- Under pressure, a resilient team shows greater flexibility and originality.
- The team sees change as less threatening.
- The team responds better to favourable feedback, makes

more positive judgments about others and other teams.

- The team contains individuals who fall sick less often.

The four things that resilient teams do

On 15 January 2009, US Airways Flight 1549 was scheduled to fly from LaGuardia Airport in New York City to Charlotte Douglas International Airport in Charlotte, North Carolina. The plane carrying 155 people made a miraculous emergency landing in the Hudson River after a bird strike disabled both engines. Through the collective expertise, quick thinking and calm demeanour of the crew, they were able to improvise a solution and successfully evacuate all passengers and crew members demonstrating teamwork, decision making and resilience in guiding the plane to a safe landing in the icy waters.

While individual resilience is undoubtedly important, the success of any endeavour often depends upon the collective resilience of the people working in teams. Just as a chain is only as strong as its weakest link, a team's effectiveness is determined by the resilience of its members and their ability to work together particularly in challenging circumstances.

Resilient teams, unlike resilient individuals, possess four key characteristics:

- Resilient teams possess **a shared belief in their collective capabilities**. Beyond individual confidence, they collectively trust in their ability to overcome challenges and achieve their goals. Team members can provide emotional support, encouragement and motivation to each other to give a shared confidence, which is a powerful force that drives resilience. However, it's important to balance confidence with a healthy dose of realism. Excessive confidence can lead to complacency, while low confidence can prevent risks from being taken.

- Within the dynamics of the team, resilient teams possess **a shared understanding of their roles and respon-sibilities**. It's crucial that this understanding is both accurate and shared among all team members. The clarity enables them to coordinate themselves effectively, to make decisions collectively and to accurately predict each other's behaviour when faced with challenges. A discrepancy in either can lead to suboptimal outcomes. For instance, a team may agree on a course of action but execute it incorrectly, or they may disagree on the best approach, causing delays and hindering progress.

- Resilient teams possess **the ability to adapt, improvise and innovate in the face of challenges**. They can think creatively, drawing on the collective strengths and past experiences of individual team members. They rely upon each other's expertise to develop effective solutions and feel more accountable for their actions

- Resilient team members **trust each other and feel safe psychologically**, meaning that they are comfortable sharing unusual or creative ideas and taking risks without fear of judgement or ridicule. When team members trust that their ideas will be valued and respected, they are more likely to share their thoughts freely, leading to better decision making and problem solving. This openness encourages a diversity of viewpoints leading them to approach solutions considering different perspectives.

The way to lead resilient teams

Team managers and team leaders can build and develop team resilience by proactively developing the four essential attributes of resilient teams: shared belief, effective teamwork, adaptability and psychological safety. This should be done proactively, anticipating potential challenges, during crises or adverse events, and in the aftermath to reinforce these qualities.

Team resilience can be built by setting clear objectives, providing relevant training, empowering teams and creating a framework for crisis response. To be effective and to maintain a positive and supportive team environment, leaders must promote a culture of mutual respect, emphasise the value of diversity and address disrespectful behaviour promptly.

In times of adversity, leaders should provide timely information and guidance for maintaining direction. They can reinforce their team's resilience by reminding team members of their past successes and capabilities, coaching team members and reframing challenges as opportunities for growth and learning.

Leaders should be an advocate for their team's needs with the organisation, ensuring they have the necessary resources and support to effectively address challenges and achieve their goals. Additionally, leaders must be adept at protecting their teams from external pressures that could hinder their progress. They should also facilitate collaboration between their teams and other departments within the organisation where appropriate.

Following a challenging event, leaders should facilitate a reflective discussion to debrief the experience. This review should focus on both successes and areas for improvement. Encourage team members to share their thoughts and concerns openly. It's essential to acknowledge and appreciate the contributions of all team members during challenging times. By recognising their efforts, leaders can boost morale, engender a sense of camaraderie and reinforce the importance of teamwork.

Resilient teams are a valuable asset to any organisation. While individual resilience is developed independently, team resilience requires deliberate cultivation by leadership. Although it may be challenging, the investment in building resilient teams pays off in the form of stronger organisations that can weather adversity and achieve long-term success.

Strengthening resilience in others

When faced with change, people undergo change in themselves and express their emotional responses in ways that are personal to them.

Some people adapt at a faster rate than others, and some change more slowly, experiencing a range of emotions much more intensely. Keep in mind that everyone reacts differently to change. Some people will readily show their emotions and be outwardly emotional, while others will experience their emotions much more internally. It's important to determine where they are emotionally as change progresses, in order that you can support them and engage with them more effectively. You should try not to judge how a person experiences change, as everyone will experience it differently according to other things that are going on in their life, their personality, their behaviour, their attitude and a whole host of other reasons.

In order to strengthen other people's resilience, consider ways to map their minds and map their hearts by considering the team overall.

Mapping the minds and hearts of teams in times of change is crucial because it enables leaders to understand the emotional and cognitive environment in which their team members are working. This understanding facilitates effective communication and supports the alignment of goals, ultimately fostering resilience and adaptability within the team during periods of transition.

In the first instance, it's important to remind them of what isn't changing, what's staying the same. Help them to understand the reasons for the change and the challenges that they're facing at an appropriate time.

It's important as well to acknowledge that people are going to experience some level of loss, so listen to people's anxieties and fears; especially listen to what their emotions are telling them and subsequently what they're telling you. Shift any negativity away from what's going wrong to what can be done to put things right.

Break down some of the larger problems and challenges into more manageable parts.

However, the most important consideration is to increase the levels of communication about the coming changes and the challenges that people are facing. There's no way that you can provide too much information and communication during change.

Engage everyone in developing a shared vision of what things can be done to create a realistic, optimistic future that everyone can share in.

Look for opportunities for them to network and increase their social connections. Teams are more productive, sustainable and resilient when members enjoy working together and being in the company of each other and their leader. Leaders are placing a greater priority on building strong bonds to improve their team's synergy.

Encourage people to have a healthy balance around their work commitments and things that are going on for them in their life elsewhere.

Celebrate little victories. These are the things that can help bring the team together.

Done well, these can increase team engagement, team responsiveness, team dynamics, and team resilience.

Building a resilient team also requires understanding both the minds and hearts of its members.

Mapping minds focuses on understanding each member's strengths, weaknesses and preferred coping mechanisms.

Mapping hearts involves acknowledging individual emotions and fostering empathy within the team to create a safe space for open communication and emotional support.

Mapping minds

- Build effective leadership.
- Establish common goals; identify targets and timetables that have a sense of urgency.
- Pay attention to building teams.
- Ensure the team is made up of the right people with the right mix of skills.
- Assign specific responsibilities to team members.

- Identify resources available to the team.
- Run meetings effectively.
- Improve communication.
- Identify key information for sharing.
- Establish rewards and incentives for all team members.
- Identify win–win solutions.
- Be competent; have clarity.
- Trust team members.
- Deliver results.
- Celebrate success and have fun.

Mapping hearts

- Work to promote friendship and camaraderie.
- Place importance on appreciation and understanding.
- Help each other through individual coaching.
- Promote a sense of togetherness.
- Learn and evolve together.
- Promote harmony.
- Reward openness.
- Pay attention to team chemistry.
- Celebrate often and put value on a positive atmosphere.
- Identify and work from the team spirit and soul.

By combining these maps, teams can make the most of individual talents, build trust and effectively navigate challenges together, ultimately strengthening their overall resilience. By acknowledging and addressing both the rational and emotional aspects of change, you can moderate any resistance and enhance overall team performance.

Strategies for developing team resilience

Empowering teams and building team resilience requires a multifaceted approach that nurtures a supportive team culture, encourages open communication and manages potential stress issues to promote cohesion and strengthen the team in challenging situations.

It's important to acknowledge that attitudes towards strategies for development may vary across organisational cultures, with some embracing them more positively than others due to differing values, traditions and approaches.

Collaboration across the organisation strengthens resilience by putting to use the diverse skills and perspectives of various people to tackle challenges more effectively.

As a leader, your behaviour and emotional management sets the tone for your team, influencing their response to challenges.

Regular communication and feedback that supports openness and transparency is necessary to encourage the sharing of challenges, concerns and successes.

Here are some action strategies for you to consider.

- Lead by example by demonstrating resilience, adaptability and a positive attitude in the face of challenges.
- Clarify roles and responsibilities to ensure that each team member understands what is expected of them within the team, as well as how their contributions are aligned with team goals and objectives. Clear expectations help reduce confusion and encourage accountability.
- Build trust and psychological safety and create an environment where team members feel safe to express

their opinions, take risks and make mistakes without fear of judgement or reprisal.

- Promote team collaboration and teamwork by creating opportunities for cross-functional team-building activities and sharing goals.
- Develop problem-solving skills by providing training and resources that empower team members; encourage a proactive approach to addressing challenges and to finding solutions collaboratively.
- Encourage adaptability and flexibility by encouraging team members to embrace change and learn from setbacks.
- Help team members develop the resilience to navigate uncertainty and ambiguity with confidence.
- Provide regular feedback that promotes continuous improvement and growth.
- Celebrate successes and milestones by recognising and celebrating team achievements, both big and small, to boost morale and reinforce a sense of accomplishment.

Here are some more unusual action strategies for strengthening resilience in teams that you might like to consider.

- Random acts of kindness. Launch a campaign where team members engage in random acts of kindness for each other or for the community. This not only boosts morale but also encourages empathy, gratitude and a sense of interconnectedness within the team.
- Reverse mentoring programmes. Implement a reverse mentoring program where junior team members mentor senior team members on topics such as technology, social media trends or new methodologies. This encourages humility, openmindedness and continuous

learning, which are important qualities for resilience in a rapidly changing world.

- Fantasy role-playing games. Organise fantasy role-playing game sessions, where team members create characters and embark on epic adventures together. This fosters creativity, teamwork and the ability to think in the moment in unpredictable scenarios.
- Silence retreats. Organise silence retreats or offsite retreats where members spend time in nature without speaking for a certain period of time. This encourages introspection, mindfulness and the development of inner resilience through solitude and reflection.

By incorporating these action strategies, teams can develop a deeper sense of resilience, adaptability and cohesion that ultimately enhances their ability to thrive in the face of ongoing challenges.

Organisational resilience

While organisations themselves don't experience emotions, their resilience hinges on the emotional resilience of the people within them. Building a resilient organisation requires considering the ability of employees to work with inevitable challenges and work through any setbacks.

Organisational resilience includes disaster recovery systems, dealing with disruption and catastrophes. Yet it also focuses on the people issues on a day-to-day basis.

Building organisational resilience depends upon two key pillars: strong core values and fostering individual resilience.

Transparent core values, meaningful to everyone inside and outside the organisation, provide clear direction and a guiding principle during challenging times. These values act as a framework for interpreting events and shaping responses. Ideally, an organisation's core values remain consistent over a long period of time, offering a dependable source of support during the good times as well as the bad times.

Leadership plays a crucial role. Leaders need to demonstrate resilience themselves and actively cultivate it within their teams. This involves identifying and addressing pressure points across the organisation to mitigate their impact. Building wellbeing and resilience assessments into the recruitment process further strengthens the foundation of a resilient workforce.

Working with volatility, uncertainty, complexity and ambiguity (VUCA)

VUCA is an acronym which is widely used today to describe or reflect on the volatility, uncertainty, complexity and ambiguity of general conditions. It's derived from military vocabulary and it came into common use in business in the 1990s. VUCA has been used in emerging ideas that apply to a wide range of organisations.

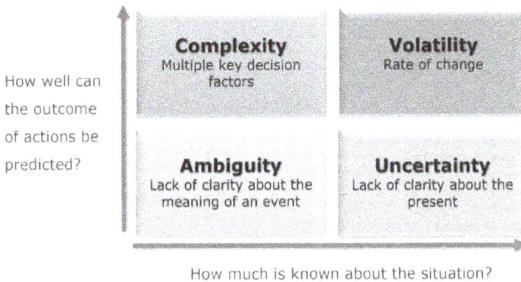

Figure 9: Volatility, uncertainty, complexity and ambiguity is related to what is known and the predicted outcomes (Bennett and Lemoine 2014).

VUCA is a practical code for awareness and readiness. The capacity for VUCA in organisations depends upon the changing nature of the technical, social, political, market and economic realities of the environments in which people work.

In every situation, how much is known and the certainty of predictions made about the outcomes of any action provide some indication of the relative degree of VUCA. If a lot is known about the situation, and a lot is known about the outcome of actions and can be predicted, then the situation is likely to be volatile. This means that it's liable to change rapidly and unpredictably, especially for the worst. Organisations that are based around delivering projects often experience delays and changes. Many unexpected events can occur and can impact on any aspect of a project.

For example, a supplier delivery arrives late or a client pushes back the approval process, negatively impacting the project schedule. These changes are volatile and regularly disrupt the normal course of activities, so leaders and teams must be able to adjust at all times. This will drive the rate of change.

If little is known about the outcome of action but a lot is known about the situation, then there's uncertainty. There's a lack of clarity about the present and what to do. The uncertainty lies in not knowing what to do and the best way forward working with all the relevant facts and details. This leads to a lack of clarity about the present, uncertainty about how to use the information to get the best outcome and uncertainty about the right way forward. This will increase risks around planning, making it difficult to forecast future needs around time, budget and human resource needs.

Of course, uncertainty can come from volatile events. In order to stay competitive, organisations must differentiate themselves and, therefore, must innovate. However, innovation itself is a process that's fraught with uncertainty. If a lot is known about the outcome of action and can be predicted, but little is known about the situation itself, then complexity is involved.

With complexity, a situation has many parts and it's difficult to understand or find an answer to how to work with the situation. Often organisations, especially small companies, work on dozens or hundreds of projects at any one time and this increases complexity. Each of these projects is assigned different resources and deadlines. Resources, project phases, deadlines are all interconnected variables that are interdependent. This means that projects and project phases depend upon each other because some tasks have to be completed before people can start the next task, and some resources depend upon other resources to carry out their activities and so on.

Moreover, there are many stakeholders involved in the execution of a project. Each of them has their own perceptions, definitions and objectives. Stakeholder management adds to the complexity and generates issues related to quality, duration, cost and performance. This drives multiple key decision factors. If little is known about the situation, and little is known about the outcome of action and can't be predicted, then there's ambiguity.

Ambiguous situations are open to more than one interpreta-tion. There's an inexactness in these circumstances which can therefore possibly cause confusion. In most working envi-ronments there's ambiguity when you must make decisions without having all the information or seeing the whole picture. Ambiguity arises if objectives are not outlined properly, when roles and responsibilities are not clearly defined or when the needs and requirements of a client are poorly understood. Communication is a recurring problem in most organisations, especially if every department uses a different communica-tion channel. This also contributes to ambiguity.

Leadership is needed to drive through an interpretation that would work and help people to understand what that means and give meaning to events.

The capacity of individuals and organisations to deal with VUCA

The capacity of individuals and organisations to deal with VUCA can be assessed and measured in several different engagement themes, which is an important focus in leadership.

Knowledge management is the key to navigating challenges effectively. It involves:

- Situational awareness: gathering and analysing information to understand the current situation, including planning and preparedness levels.
- Data-driven decision making: analysing the potential impact of decisions through various models that consider how they would affect people.
- Optimised processes: ensuring efficient workflows and utilising the right resources for the task at hand.
- Effective response: reacting to situations in a practical and functional manner.
- Continuous improvement: learning from past failures, both systematic and behavioural, to identify areas for improvement and foster a positive learning environment.
- Recovery and adaptation: implementing robust systems and practices to help individuals, teams and the entire organisation move forward after challenges.

Beyond the simple acronym is a whole body of knowledge that deals with leadership models and learning models for

VUCA. These include being prepared, anticipating, evolving and intervening. So as a leader, it's important to understand how people are working, leading them to be prepared to anticipate the future, to evolve as the situation changes and to put the right interventions in place.

Being emotionally intelligent enables leaders to effectively navigate and adapt to rapidly changing circumstances while maintaining stability and fostering resilience within their teams.

Emotionally intelligent leaders recognise and manage the emotions driving the climate in which people are operating. They empathise with others' perspectives and inspire confidence and trust. In so doing, leaders using their emotional intelligence well can maintain composure, make rational decisions amid any chaos, encourage and motivate their teams, and foster a more cohesive and adaptable organisational culture in turbulent, ever-changing situations.

Ways to build resilient organisations

Resilient organisations are built by:

- designing effective corporate governance
- assessing vulnerabilities
- planning for a range of scenarios and outcomes
- developing an up-to-date business continuity plan
- creating teams of people by mapping their minds and mapping their hearts
- responding proactively.

It's interesting how many organisations didn't have the resilience to withstand the coronavirus pandemic of the early 2020s. They'd not been built to withstand such a severe catastrophe. This may seem extreme, but it's a scenario that should have been considered and planned for, however unlikely.

The question to consider is *'What is the worst that could happen?'*.

In contemplating the answer, a further question should have been asked – *'What is even worse?'* – and then the organisation should have started to plan for that. This is how organisations work effectively to be resilient under any circumstances.

As mentioned, it may seem extreme, but as has been proved, these extreme cases do occur.

A resilient culture is developed by ensuring that there are management resources:

- for developing foresight to anticipate major events and change
- to establish a planning process that effectively translates the organisation's strategy into actionable plans
- to develop teams by mapping hearts and mapping minds.

People are the most expensive commodity within an organisation. It's the people who create the organisation. In developing organisational resilience, people will be aligned with the organisation's values and strategy and give their full commitment to the business, which is a fundamental part of giving the organisation the resilience that it needs for the long term.

Action strategies to develop resilience

Feel in control

- View the world as complex and challenging, but filled with opportunity.
- Hold a positive perception about yourself.
- Defend yourself well.
- Be confident in your ability to meet any challenge with hope and realistic optimism.

Emotions that drain and stop you from feeling in control are *hopelessness*, *discomfort* and *disappointment*.

Emotions that facilitate you feeling in control are *esteem*, *contentment* and *optimism*.

- Be realistic about what you can and can't do.
- Learn how to say 'no' so that you don't commit to too much.
- Challenge your own self-limiting beliefs.
- Set small, short-term goals that you know you can achieve.
- Tell yourself you can do it and prove yourself to be right.
- Communicate your intentions clearly to others, delegate and encourage their support.

Create a personal vision

- Know what you believe in.
- Have a clear vision of what you want to accomplish and achieve.
- Approach adversity and stress with a sense of hope.
- Let your belief and purpose carry you forward in life.

Emotions that drain and stop you from creating a personal vision are *frustration*, *inadequacy* and *anxiety*.

Emotions that facilitate creating a personal vision are *esteem*, *engagement* and *passion*.

- Set yourself clear goals and objectives focusing on what you want to achieve.
- Establish a plan that will accomplish your goals.
- Ensure that the plan is made up of small, achievable steps.
- Remain committed, even if events take you away from your plan for a short while.
- Remind yourself of what you want to achieve and why.
- Challenge your own self-limiting beliefs.

Be flexible and adaptable

- Be sensitive to changes in your environment.
- Adapt quickly to what is happening.
- Learn from life constantly.
- Remain true to your purpose or vision while making room for other's ideas and opportunities.

Emotions that drain and stop you from being flexible and adaptable are *fear*, *disappointment* and *anxiety*.

Emotions that facilitate you being flexible and adaptable are *esteem*, *contentment* and *optimism*.

- Anticipate change so that you can be prepared for it with a series of contingencies.
- Accept that situations are going to change.
- Positively move forward rather than dwelling on how unreasonable or unfair the changes may seem.
- Remain focused on your personal goals and adapt how you work to accommodate the change.

Get organised

- Create structures and methods for bringing order and stability on your terms.
- Set realistic goals for yourself.
- Expect things to work out.
- Manage the moment with calmness and clarity of purpose.

Emotions that drain and stop you from getting organised are *hopelessness*, *fear* and *discomfort*.

Emotions that facilitate you getting organised are *esteem*, *pride* and *enthusiasm*.

- Create a plan or draw up a list of tasks.
- Create systems and processes that make you efficient.
- Be realistic about how you can manage your time.
- Avoid putting off anything that eventually needs to be done.
- Tackle big projects by breaking them down into smaller chunks and start to work on them one chunk at a time.
- Be aware of, and avoid, anything that you find distracting.

A mindset for problem solving

- Think critically, creatively and reflectively.
- View seemingly impossible problems as challenges and opportunities for learning and growth.
- View failures as opportunities for inspiration.
- Collaborate with others.
- Anticipate setbacks and mishaps.
- Solve problems for the long term.

Emotions that drain and stop you from problem solving are *anger*, *hurt* and *guilt*.

Emotions that facilitate you problem solving are *engagement*, *contentment* and *happiness*.

- Gather as much information about the issue as possible.
- Define the problem precisely and accurately.
- Evaluate it objectively.
- Look at the problem from different perspectives.
- Generate a number of options drawings from your experience and the experience of others.
- Critically review the options and decide what will work.
- Be decisive and start to put agreed plans into action.

Get connected

- Reach out to others.
- Contribute to others' welfare by giving of yourself.
- Build bridges.
- Discover common ground.
- Be playful and creative when exploring opportunities together.
- Touch each other's hearts.

Emotions that drain and stop you from getting connected are *loneliness*, *anger* and *sadness*

Emotions that facilitate you getting connected are *engagement*, *love* and *contentment*.

- Look for new opportunities to build your network.
- Proactively seek out the chance to engage with different people.
- Communicate with empathy.
- Listen.
- Look at ways you can get involved and help others with their problems.
- Be willing to seek support for yourself.

Be socially competent

- Have good relationships and social interactions.
- Seek out others' perspectives.
- Demonstrate empathy and an understanding for others.
- Share your feelings honestly.
- Laugh at yourself.

Emotions that drain and stop you from being socially competent are *guilt*, *loneliness* and *hurt*.

Emotions that facilitate you being socially competent are *love*, *happiness* and *passion*.

- Evaluate your existing network to ensure that you can draw upon a variety of backgrounds, skills and experience.
- Keep an open mind to broaden your horizons.
- Be selective about the support you need.
- Ask people for help on both practical and emotional levels.
- Enjoy humour as a part of your social interactions.

Be proactive

- Engage change directly.
- Focus on – and expand – your sphere of influence.
- Focus on what actions you can take versus waiting for others to act.
- Experience and celebrate small victories.
- Lead others through change by setting an example.

Emotions that drain and stop you from being proactive are *frustration*, *hopelessness* and *inadequacy*.

Emotions that facilitate you being proactive are *enthusiasm*, *esteem* and *pride*.

- Use your foresight to plan ahead and prioritise.
- Critically evaluate how tasks can be completed more efficiently.
- Act decisively.
- Keep on top of the less urgent tasks.
- Identify and develop the skills that you will need for the future.
- Don't waste time on truly unnecessary tasks.
- Take the lead and become a role model for others.

The Paradox of Resilience

At your worst times you can become your best.

Resilience is forged through adversity, not despite it.

Bibliography

Aburn, G, Gott, M & Hoare, K (2016) 'What is resilience? An integrative review of the empirical literature'. *Journal of Advanced Nursing* 72(5), 980–1000.

Bennett, N & Lemoine, J (2014) 'What VUCA really means for you'. *Harvard Business Review* 92.

Coutu, D L (2002) 'How resilience works'. *Harvard Business Review* 80(5), 46–50, 52, 55.

Davidson R J (2004) 'What does the prefrontal cortex "do" in affect: Perspectives in frontal EEG asymmetry research'. *Biological Psychology* 67, 219–34.

Davidson R.J with Begley S (2012) *The Emotional Life of your Brain*. Hodder and Stoughton.

Fisher, J M (2000) 'Creating the future?' in Scheer, J W (ed), *The Person in Society: Challenges to a Constructivist Theory*. Psychosozial-Verlag.

Hartwig, A, Clarke, S et al (2020) 'Workplace team resilience: A systematic review and conceptual development'. *Organizational Psychology Review* 10(3–4), 169–200.

Kim, M J & Whalen, P J (2009) 'The structural integrity of an amygdala-prefrontal pathway predicts trait anxiety". *Journal of Neuroscience* 29 11614–8.

Kirkman, B, Stoverink, A C et al (2019) 'The 4 things resilient teams do'. *Harvard Business Review.* URL: hbr.org/2019/07/the-4-things-resilient-teams-do

Kübler-Ross, E & Kessler, D (2005) *On Grief and Grieving: Finding the meaning of grief through the five stages of loss.* Simon & Schuster.

Nielsen, K, Nielsen, M B et al (2017) 'Workplace resources to improve both employee well-being and performance: A systematic review and meta-analysis'. *Work & Stress* 31(11), 1–20.

Robertson, I T & Flint-Taylor, J (2009) 'Leadership, psychological well-being and organizational outcomes' in Cartwright, S & Cooper, C (eds), *The Oxford Handbook of Organizational Well-Being.* Oxford University Press, pp. 159–79.

Rutter, M (1993) 'Resilience: Some conceptual considerations'. *Journal of Adolescent Health,* 14(8), 626-31.

Seligman, M E P (2006) *Learned Optimism: How to change your mind and your life.* Vintage Books.

Shatte, A, Perlman, A et al (2017) 'The positive effect of resilience on stress and business outcomes in difficult work environments'. *Journal of Occupational and Environmental Medicine* 59(2), 135–140.

Taleb, N N (2012) *Antifragile: Things that gain from disorder.* Allen Lane.

Yerkes, R M & Dodson, J D (1908) 'The relation of strength of stimulus to rapidity of habit-formation'. *Journal of Comparative Neurology and Psychology* 18, 459–82.

Acknowledgements

Building resilience, both personal and for this book, requires all the action strategies highlighted in the chapter *Action strategies to develop resilience*. With particular reference to 'Get connected' and 'Be socially competent', I would like to acknowledge a number of key people who, like sturdy oaks that weather storms, provided unwavering support throughout the time I worked on the book.

Elevated from the final mention in the first edition to primary acknowledgement in this edition is my wife, Helen. She spent many happy hours preparing the manuscript for review from the original book, audio and video files.

Special mention must go to John Fisher who has been very encouraging of my interpretations of his Personal Transition through Change curve that makes up a major part of the book. I met him a few times before the first edition was published and over the years we have become firm friends.

Thanks go to Udemy, Coursera, SkillSuccess, Alison, Cornerstone/CyberU, LearnFormula and Michael Management as well as other online learning platforms for hosting and supporting my emotional intelligence, stress management and resilience courses. The online course based on this book alone has been taken by over 10,000 learners. Feedback from many of the unnamed students has helped me to refine and develop the ideas over the years.

Thank you to Natasha Trobbiani, from Córdoba, Argentina, who co-instructed a resilience course with me on Udemy. Her input to this course has expanded my knowledge of resilience. I do hope that we get to meet in person someday.

My thanks extend to RSVP Design for their support around the coaching toolbox Images of Resilience, which we developed together in 2011. This commercially available experiential training resource has been an integral part of my resilience workshops over the years. I have gained many insights around resilience and have heard some wonderful personal stories through the cathartic conversations stimulated by the images.

Special gratitude goes to Kasper Moller Christiansen, who has been working on my behalf to get me featured on some of the largest and most influential business and lifestyle podcasts. His persistence in the promotion of my books ensures that they reach a global audience. I would also like to thank the many host podcasters who have given me the opportunity to talk about my books on their shows and for insisting that I promote them to their audiences.

Of course, none of this would be possible without The Right Book Press team led by Sue Richardson. They have been instrumental in guiding and advising me about getting the books to market. Without them this book would never have been published.

About the author

Robin Hills, Doctor of Advanced Studies – Psychology (*honoris causa*), is director of Ei4Change (Emotional Intelligence 4 Change) a multi-award-winning company specialising in training, coaching and personal development focused on emotional intelligence, positive psychology and neuroscience. Ei4Change have become recognised as the established experts on making emotional intelligence practical and applicable, particularly within business settings.

In 2024, Robin was awarded an honorary doctorate from Azteca Universidad in recognition of his lifetime work in helping people to develop their emotional intelligence and resilience.

Robin has over 40 years' business and commercial experience working with leaders and executives to develop their performance through increased self-awareness and understanding of others. His clients include small start-ups through to large multinational companies, the public sector (including the NHS) and charities.